Table of Contents

A Food Trip from Sicily To Taipei

If You Cannot Travel, You Can Taste It – From Sicily To Taipei

BY: Ida Smith

License Notes

Introduction

Have you ever wondered how traveling for food feels like? We are about to take one, so come along with us! We will journey through lands that you probably do not know, having delicious and unique cooking methods that will wow your taste buds. From Sicily to Taipei, they are recipes that will make you a remarkable chef.

Infamous Taipei Mango Shaved Ice

Everyone loves mango, and this Taiwanese version is one for keeping.

Total Prep Time: 35 minutes

Yield: 2

Ingredient List:

- 1 can condensed milk
- 2 cups ripe mango cubes
- 2 tbsp sugar
- Juice of ½ lemon
- Ice

Preparation:

Blend the mango cubes and sieve.
Boil the mango pulp with sugar until thickened.
Stir in the lemon juice. Then, set aside.
In a bowl of shaved ice, add some mango cubes, the mango puree, and milk.
Serve cold.

Laap Gai Salad

This is a minced meat salad usually found on the streets of Laos.

Total Prep Time: 30 minutes

Yield: 4

Ingredient List:

- 1 small red onion sliced
- 2 cups lettuces
- 1 cup shredded carrots
- 1 tbsp chopped mints
- 400g spicy cooked chicken
- 1 slice lemon
- More mints for garnish
- A dash of black pepper

Preparation:
Chop the lettuce and add them to the bowl.
Add the rest of the rest ingredients and sprinkle the black pepper.
Serve with a slice of lemon.

Prezganka (Scramble Egg Soup)

This flour dish is not the most appealing, but it is delicious and filling. It is a great way to get the required nutrients, especially during winter.

Total Prep Time: 45 minutes

Yield: 2

Ingredient List:

- 2 eggs
- ½ cup flour
- 1.5 l soup bass
- 90g butter
- Salt and pepper
- ½ tsp cumin powder
- 1 cup shredded carrot
- Mint for garnish

Preparation:
Melt the butter and cook the flour and cumin until brown.
Add the carrots and gradually add the soup base and water to loosen the roux.
Whisking hard, add the remaining liquid and bring it to a boil.
Add the beaten egg to scramble.
Season and serve.

Chinese Sweet and Sour Pork Tenderloin

This classic Cantonese recipe has been repeated all over the world, but it still retains its two-tone taste.

Yield: 3

Total Prep Time:s 40 minutes

Ingredient List:

- 200g pork tenderloin strips
- 1 large egg
- A handful of coriander
- 2 tbsp tomato paste
- 1 tsp sugar
- 1 yellow and red pepper chopped
- 1 tbsp soy sauce
- 2 tsp corn starch divided
- ¼ cup canola oil
- Salt as desired
- 10g rice wine vinegar

Preparation:

Separate the egg white and yolk.

In a bowl containing the egg white, add corn starch, soy sauce, and salt the bowl.

Add the pork strips to the bowl and allow it to sit for 20 minutes.

In yet another bowl, mix the remaining starch, vinegar with a little water to make the slurry.

Fry the marinated pork in the oil and sugar mixture until crisp and set aside.

Add the tomato paste, pepper, and more water, simmer and then add the cried pork.

Stir in the slurry and allow it to cook until thick and shiny.

Sicilian Spaghetti Ai Ricci

This elegant dish is your regular pasta cooked with sea urchins. It is very simple, no hard work, just big flavors and creaminess.

Total Prep Time: 30 minutes

Yield: 4

Ingredient List:

- 500g spaghetti
- 4 tbsp extra virgin olive oil
- 4 cloves garlic, smashed and chopped
- 1 red chili chopped
- 2 tbsp chopped parsley
- 12 large sea urchins
- Salt to taste

Preparation:
Cut open and scoop the urchins' flesh out into a bowl.
Cook the pasta according to the instructions.
Meanwhile, sauté the garlic chili under low heat.
Drain the pasta and set ½ cup of pasta water aside.
Add the urchin eggs to the oil and sauté for 30 seconds and add the pasta.
Toss well, season, and serve with parsley garnish.

Taipei crispy Chicken cutlets

Everyone loves chicken. Whether you are in Sicily or Taipei, it does not matter. However, well-cooked chicken is all that matters.

Total Prep Time: 30 minutes

Yield: 4

Ingredient List:

- 8 pieces chicken thighs boneless and skinless
- 1 tsp garlic powder
- 1 tsp chili flakes
- 1 tsp black pepper
- 1 tsp cumin
- 1 tbsp soy sauce
- Salt to taste
- 1 cup panko crumbs
- ½ cup coconut flour
- 1 large egg white beaten
- Oil for frying

Preparation:
Season the chicken with salt and pepper. Then, set aside.
Mix the egg white with the soy sauce in a bowl.
Next, in another bowl, mix the panko, coconut flour, chili flakes, cumin, and salt.
Heat up the oil until shimmering.
Then, evenly dip the chicken in the egg white and panko mix and into the oil.
Repeat until done and serve.

Not Ratatouille but Caponata

This is a healthy dish that pairs beautifully with seafood or alone. It is fresh, vibrant and delicious.

Total Prep Time: 50 minutes

Yield: 4

Ingredient List:

- 2 tbsp red wine
- 2 tbsp olive oil
- ¼ cup raisins dried
- 250g purple eggplant
- 1 large red and yellow bell pepper chopped
- 2 shallots chopped
- 2 Roma tomatoes chopped
- 2 tbsp chopped capers
- 1 red chili chopped
- 3 sprigs chopped mint
- 1 dozen scalloped cleaned
- Salt & pepper

Preparation:

Season the scallops with salt and pepper.
Pour the oil into a pan, seared the scallops for 2-3 minutes.
Remove from the oil and set aside; add the raisin into the red wine to make them succulent.
In the same pan, add the eggplant, shallots, peppers and cook until soft.
Stir in the tomatoes, capers, and spices with the red wine and raisins.
Cook down for 2 minutes, add the scallops and serve.

Spicy Sweet Taipei Chicken Feet

These chicken feet are a delicacy, you may not like their appearance, but they are good.

Total Prep Time: 40 minutes

Yield: 4

Ingredient List:

- 2 dozen chicken feet cleaned
- 1 tbsp brown sugar
- 2 tbsp soy sauce
- 1 tsp garlic minced
- 2 Serrano chilies
- Salt and pepper
- 2 tsp tomato paste

Preparation:

Cook the chicken in just enough water and salt until soft and stick.
If the liquid dries up, add some more.
Add the rest of the ingredients. Then, allow to cook some more.
Serve with a sprinkle of sesame seeds.

Spicy breaded Fried Sardines

Sicily is an island surrounded by plenty of fresh produce from the sea. Sardine is the most popular, and these are just right.

Total Prep Time: 15 minutes

Yield: 5

Ingredient List:

- 5 medium-sized sardines butterflied and deboned
- 1 tsp cayenne
- 1 tsp chili flakes
- 1 cup coconut flour
- Salt and pepper
- Oil to fry

Preparation:

Mix the spices, salt, pepper, and flour in a bowl.
Towel-dry the sardines, season with salt and pepper.
Drenched with the flour.
Shake the excess and fry until crisp.
Serve.

Taipei Pineapple Cake

This is not your regular pineapple cake. It is a mouthful of deliciousness that melts in your mouth with every bite.

Total Prep Time: 40 minutes
Yield: 8

Ingredient List:

- 700g freshly chopped pineapple
- 150g sugar
- ½ tsp ginger finely grated
- 600g store-bought shortcrust dough

Preparation:

Squeeze any excess juice using cheesecloth.

Add the pulp to a pot and caramelize with the sugar, 100g of the juice, and ginger, and cook until no liquid is left.

Scoop into a bowl and set aside to cool down.

Take a piece of the dough, make it into a ball, then flatten, scoop a spoonful to the middle, fold and squeeze into a square cutter.

Repeat until done, and then bake for 15 -20 minutes.

It should be brown and flaky.

Cheesy Rosemary Foccacia Bread

Sicily is in Italy; it will only be fair to give a little of the country where it originates from. Foccacia is a delicious loaf that makes the perfect complement to soups, stews and even sandwiches.

Total Prep Time: 2 hours

Yield: 1

Ingredient List:

- 500g bread flour
- 2 tbsp salt
- 150g parmesan cheese
- 1 tbsp black pepper
- 1 sachet active dry yeast
- 1 ¾ cups warm water
- ¼ cup olive oil
- Fresh rosemary sprig

Preparation:
Proof the yeast with the warm water
Add the flour, parmesan, salt, pepper, and oil to make a smooth dough
Cover to proof beat down and knead, cover to proof again
Beat down and form into the shape and allow it to prove some more
The more you proof and knead, the softer the dough
Oil a large baking tray. Then, place the dough on it, poke holes and insert the rosemary
Drizzle more olive oil over and bake until brown
Serve

Spicy Fried Shrimps with Salted Cashew nuts

Some foods actually look too good to eat, and this is one of them, too.

Total Prep Time: 10 minutes

Yield: 2

Ingredient List:

- 2 dozen shrimps, cleaned
- 1 tbsp soy sauce
- 1 tbsp sweet chili
- 1 tsp red chili chopped
- ½ cup roasted salted cashew nuts
- 1 tbsp scallion chopped
- 1 tsp garlic
- ½ tsp ginger
- 2 tbsp sesame oil
- 1 tsp Sichuan pepper

Preparation:

Add half the sesame oil to a wok and sauté the chili, ginger, and garlic for 60 seconds. Add the cashews and shrimps with the remaining ingredients except for the scallions. Cook until the shrimps are pink. Then, serve with the scallions.

Cambodian's Spicy Fish Amok

This is a country whose food is as diverse as the people. From rich, sweet, spicy, and sour to simple, delicate, and yummy food, Amok is a dish you will find anywhere there.

Total Prep Time: 80 minutes

Yield: 4

Ingredient List:

- 16 pieces red snapper boneless
- 500ml coconut milk
- 1/3 cup curry paste
- ¼ cup chili-garlic paste
- 1 tbsp palm sugar
- 2 tbsp fish sauce
- 2 tbsp soy sauce
- 1 tbsp canola oil
- 4 eggs
- Kaffir lime and julienned red chili to garnish

Preparation:

In a large oven bowl lined with banana leaves, arrange the fish at the base.

Whisk the coconut milk, curry paste, chili-garlic paste, and the rest of the ingredients except the garnish in a bowl.

Pour the mixture over the fish. Then, cover with another leaf and cook for 50 minutes.

Serve with garnish and rice.

Easy homemade Cannoli Shells

This crunchy and creamy snack is the perfect way to enjoy the ambiance of Italy. It can be anything you want it to be –from sweet to savory.

Total Prep Time: 30 minutes

Yield: 24

Ingredient List:

- 2 cups cake flour
- 1 cup all-purpose flour
- 1 tbsp rum
- ¼ cup powdered sugar
- 120g shortening
- 1 large egg + extra egg for egg washing
- 1 tbsp honey
- 1/8 tsp nutmeg
- 1/8 tsp cinnamon
- Salt
- Coldwater as desired
- Oil for frying

Preparation:

First, mix all the ingredients in a mixer except the oil and water
Add the water a little at a time until the dough is formed
Next, roll out the dough as thinly as possible and cut out into an oval shape
Fold round a cannoli rod and apply the egg wash at the edges to seal it by pressing hard
Then, deep fry until golden and crisp
Fill with filling of choice

Louvi Buttery Black Eye-Beans

This recipe can be cooked anyhow you want, and it is simple and delicious and keeps well too.

Total Prep Time: 40 minutes

Yield: 2

Ingredient List:

- 1 cup black-eyed beans
- 1 tbsp butter
- 200g spinach
- Salt
- 1 red chili divide
- 500g vegetable stock

Method

In a slow cooker, place all the ingredients and set on high without the spinach.
Add them when the beans are cook and soft.
Serve with some lemon wedges.

Austria's Topfentascherl

Curd filled doughs are everywhere, but this Austria variety is delicious and worth the long queues.

Total Prep Time: 30 minutes

Yield: 12

Ingredient List:

- 2 sheets Viennese Danish dough
- ½ cup black currant soaked in 1 tsp rum
- 100g cream cheese
- ¼ cup powdered sugar
- 1 cup ricotta cheese
- 2 egg yolks
- ½ tsp vanilla extract

Preparation:

Crunch the black currants and rum in a bowl and set aside.
Whip the cream, sugar, egg yolks, vanilla and fold in the ricotta in a bowl.
Roll the dough and cut into diamond shapes.
Scoop the ricotta filling and a dollop of the rum mix.
Pinch the two opposite ends like a windmill.
Allow it to double in size, brush with egg, and bake.
Serve with ice cream.

Spicy Grilled Halloumi

Although it can be eaten raw, grilled or soaked in tomato sauce with olives gives this dish an intensely rich flavor.

Total Prep Time: 10 minutes

Yield: 2

Ingredient List:

- 1 tsp oregano
- ½ tsp black pepper
- 1 tsp olive oil
- 4 1" slices Halloumi

Preparation:

Season the Halloumi cheese with the ingredients.
Place on a grill and cook 2-3 minutes on both sides.
Serve as desired.

Sweet and Buttery Spargel

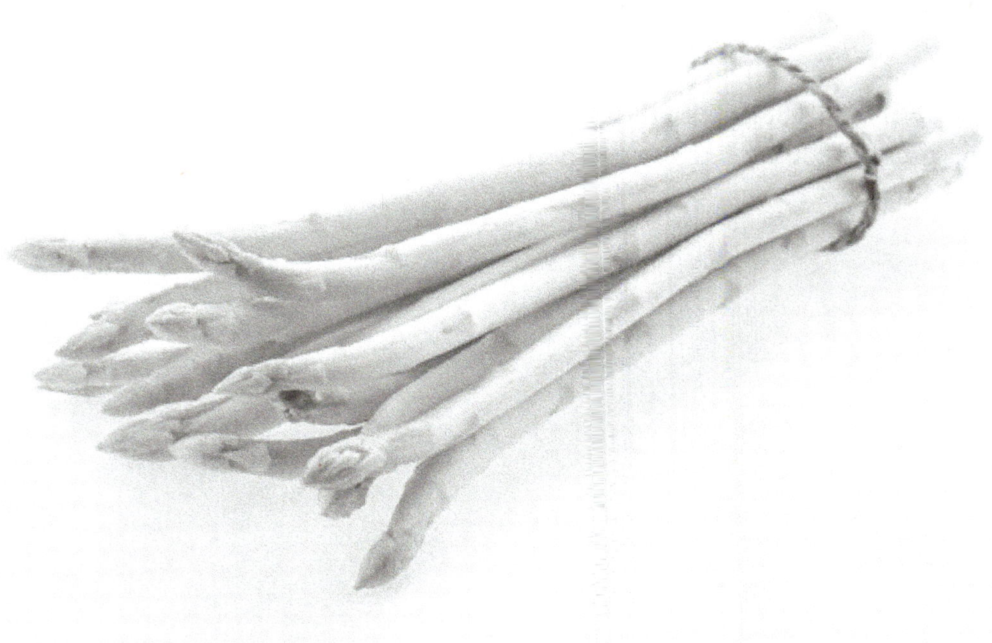

Austria is now for its beautiful asparagus, especially the white ones. This simple recipe is the perfect side dish for fish or potatoes.

Total Prep Time: 20 minutes

Yield: 2

Ingredient List:

- 1 bunch white asparagus
- 1 tbsp butter
- 1 tbsp bacon fat
- 1 tsp sugar
- 1 tbsp chopped chives
- Salt and pepper

Preparation:

Snip the tips off and peel the bark to make them look fine.

Line a baking tray spread the asparagus, and pour the mixture of melted butter, chives, sugar and bacon fat over it.

Salt and pepper as desired and cook.

Serve.

Kuwait Gers Ogaily

This traditional yellow cake gets its color from the saffron threads. It is sweet and delicious but still pairs well with whipped cream, ice creams, or even yogurts.

Total Prep Time: 50 minutes

Yield: 6

Ingredient List:

- 2 cups cake flour
- 7.5g baking powder
- 10 saffron threads + 1 tbsp sugar
- 300g sugar
- 4 eggs
- ½ cup melted butter unsalted
- 1 cup full cream milk
- 1 tsp cardamom
- 1/8 cup rose water
- ¼ cup toasted sesame seeds

Preparation:

Use the sugar to grind the saffron thread; then add half the milk to soak.

Next, mix the flour, baking powder, and half the sesame seed in a bowl.

In a mixer bowl, whisk the eggs and sugar until double and light, and add the cardamom, rose water, butter, and remaining milk.

Next, gradually fold the dry ingredients into the wet ingredients until a soft batter is formed.

Butter the pan, spread the sesame seed, and pour the batter.

Bake until done and serve with tea or warm milk.

Slovenia Yota

This hearty and delicious stew uses ingredients available in winter to create a mouthwatering delicacy. To enjoy, cook it slow and low until the beans are soft and almost melting.

Total Prep Time: 6 hours

Yield: 4

Ingredient List:

- 1 cup peeled and chopped turnips
- 500g pickled cabbage
- 500g potatoes, washed and cut into cubes
- 2 cups kidney beans, soaked overnight
- 1 cup shallots
- 2 tbsp olive oil
- 1 tsp garlic minced
- 250g smoked cured pork cubed
- 2 tbsp tomato paste
- 700ml vegetable stock
- Salt and pepper

Preparation:

Add the oil to the slow cooker. Then, sauté the shallots and garlic.

Add the tomato paste, fry for 2 minutes, add the pork, potatoes, beans, and stock.

Season accordingly and replace the lid.

Cook overnight to enable the flavor to come together.

Caramel Luqaimat

This puffy fried bun is eaten during festivals or ceremonies. When you start eating it you cannot stop, it is so delicious.

Total Prep Time: 50 minutes
Yield: 6

Ingredient List:

- 2 cups flour
- 1 tbsp vanilla custard powder
- 1 tbsp sugar
- 1 tbsp butter melted
- 1 tsp yeast
- 1 tsp baking powder
- ¼ tsp cardamom powder
- 1 ½ cups warm water
- Oil for frying
- ½ cup date syrup
- ½ cup caramel sauce

Preparation:

Activate the yeast in warm water, oil, and sugar.
Add the flour, custard, baking powder, and spice.
Mix to form a sticky dough.
Set aside to proof and then heat up the oil.
Fry into small balls.
Mix the date syrup and caramel.
Drizzle all over and serve.

Croatia Crin Rizot

Croatia Crin Rizot or black risotto is a popular Croatian delight that uses real cuttlefish ink to color the rice. While it is not the most appealing, the taste is divine.

Total Prep Time: 30 minutes

Yield: 4

Ingredient List:

- 2 cups Arborio rice
- 1 tbsp cuttlefish ink (or more if you want it darker)
- ¼ cup olive oil
- 1 small onion diced
- 1 red chili died
- 1 small carrot shredded
- ½ cup grated parmesan
- 1 tsp garlic
- 1 cup stock
- ¼ cup white wine
- Salt & white pepper

Preparation:

Rinse the rice under a running tap.
Warm the stock and set it close by.
Add the oil and sauté the onion, garlic, chili, and carrots.
Add the rice and ink, gradually ladle the stock into the rice while stirring it.
Repeat until cooked, add the parmesan and wine, and season accordingly.
Serve with seafood.

Walima Saloona

This hearty dish is a delicacy in most Arab states, especially Qatar. You can add any type of protein and vegetables as the case may be.

Total Prep Time: 100 minutes

Yield: 4

Ingredient List:

- 600g chicken boneless
- 2 cups skinless tomato chopped
- 1 large onion chopped
- ½ tsp garlic minced
- 1 1" piece ginger grated
- 150g potatoes hunks
- 1 cup carrot chunks
- 2 tbsp tomato paste
- 1 tsp turmeric
- 1 dry lemon broken into pieces
- ¼ cup deseeded red chili
- 1 tsp cumin, ¼ tsp cardamom, ½ tsp Arab spice mix
- 1 cinnamon stick
- ¼ cup oil

Preparation:

Boil the chicken in 200ml of water with the spices and keep the stock.

Sauté the onion, ginger, and chili.

Add the tomatoes, tomatoes paste, potatoes, carrot, and the rest ingredients into the pan.

Pour in the chicken stock and meat.

Cook on low for 30 minutes and season accordingly.

Serve.

Seafood Na Buzaru

Buzaru is a cooking method where the seafood is cooked in their shell and eaten with your hands. This very easy recipe has all your favorite aquatic creatures in one place.

Total Prep Time: 30 minutes

Yield: 4

Ingredient List:

- 1 tbsp chopped French tarragon
- 1 dozen scampi, cleaned
- 1 dozen shrimps cleaned
- 1 dozen Prawns cleaned
- 1 dozen mussels clean
- 1 large lobster, cleaned and broken down
- 1 tbsp garlic
- 1 small chili chopped
- 6 sweet cherry tomatoes sliced
- ¼ cup olive oil
- 1 small onion chopped
- 500ml white wine
- 1 cup bread crumbs

Preparation:
Sauté the onion and garlic with chili.
Add the seafood and toss in the hot oil for 2 minutes.
Add the rest of the ingredients and cook until it is cooked.
Season accordingly and serve with the tomatoes.

Laos Jaew Dipping Sauce

A perfect sauce with everything grilled, this simple sauce will add the finishing touch to all your meat dishes.

Total Prep Time: 5 minutes

Yield: 1

Ingredient List:

- ¼ cup fish sauce
- ¼ cup soy sauce
- 2 tbsp diced shallots
- 1 tbsp cane sugar
- 1 tbsp tamarind paste
- 1 tbsp Khai Hua
- 3 tbsp chopped coriander
- 1 red chili finely chopped
- 1 small lime juiced

Preparation:

Add all the ingredients to the bowl. Then, mix.
You can add a little water to reduce the intensity.
Serve.

Hungarian Beef Goulash

This is a simple and delicious sauce that can be replicated anyhow you want it.

Total Prep Time: 200 minutes

Yield: 4

Ingredient List:

- 1 l chicken stock
- 1.5kg boneless beef pieces
- 2 tbsp oil
- 2 cups carrots
- 2 cups sliced yellow and red pepper
- 1 cup chopped onion & ½ cup celery chopped
- 1 red chili chopped
- 1 tsp garlic
- 60g Hungarian paprika
- 2 tbsp tomato paste
- 1 tbsp soy sauce
- 2 bay leaves
- 1 tbsp dried thyme
- ¼ cup flour
- 2 tbsp red wine vinegar
- Parsley for garnish
- Salt and pepper

Preparation:

Season and brown beef in oil then set aside.

Sauté the onion, garlic, peppers, carrot, celery, and chili until soft.

Add the tomato paste, paprika, and flour, cook for 2-3 minutes.

Pour the stock, vinegar and return the beef, and add the bay leaves and thyme.

Cover to cook until the beef is falling apart.

Adjust the seasoning and serve.

Kangkep Baob

Kangkep Baob or stuffed frogs are a delicacy found on every street corner and in every home in Cambodia. This is our take, and it is yum!

Total Prep Time: 50 minutes

Yield: 4

Ingredient List:

- 4 large frogs
- 100g minced frog meat
- 50g peanuts
- 1 chili chopped
- 200g minced chicken
- ½ cup Kroeung spice mix
- Oil for frying
- Salt and pepper

Preparation:

Mix the kroeung spice with the minced chicken and frog meat.
Season accordingly and stuff the frogs.
Seal with a bamboo skewer and cook over a hot coal flame.
Allow it to cook until brown and puffy and soft to the touch.
Serve.

Deep Fried Langos

Not all bread is baked; some are steamed, roasted and grilled, and this is fried. Langos is crunchy but soft and beautiful.

Total Prep Time: 60 minutes

Yield: 12

Ingredient List:

- 320g all-purpose flour
- 9g yeast
- 270ml water
- ½ tsp salt
- Oil for frying

Preparation:

Dissolve the salt in water and add it to the flour and yeast mixture in a bowl.
Knead the dough continuously until a firm dough is formed and allow it to proof.
Roll out the dough. Then, using a cookie cutter, cut out 4-inch rounds.
Allow each circle to proof before frying in hot oil.
It is served with cheese, garlic and sour cream.

Pounded Egg Plant

This super healthy dip is great with potatoes, chips and yams. You can use any type of aubergine and spice to make it your own.

Total Prep Time: 30 minutes

Yield: 1

Ingredient List:

- 300g purple eggplants
- 1 red chili
- 3 cloves garlic roasted
- 1 stalk green scallion
- 12 sprigs cilantro
- 1 small shallot
- 1 tsp fish sauce
- Salt to taste

Preparation:

Grill the eggplants over an open flame.
When it is soft, pound in a mortar with the rest of the ingredients.
Adjust the seasoning and serve.

Cherry Soup Meggyleves

It is a soup made with cherries. You can consider it a warm but unique dessert, say the least and taste absolutely divine chilled.

Total Prep Time: 30 minutes

Yield: 4

Ingredient List:

- 1kg sour pitted cherries
- 1 cup sugar
- 1 vanilla pod
- ½ cup coconut flour
- 2 l sour cream

Preparation:

Cook the cherries with sugar and vanilla for 5 minutes.
Add the water and stir in the flour.
Cook until thick, add the remaining water and whisk in the sour cream.
Allow it to simmer on low heat, then serve or refrigerate until cold.
Serve.

Conclusion

Wow, they are some food adventures! Whether in Sicily or Taipei, food is a uniting factor for everyone who visits any countries. We hope they will make you explore foods around the world and make them for your family.

www.ingramcontent.com/pod-product-compliance
Lightning Source LLC
LaVergne TN
LVHW081320110826
845149LV00006B/1558
9781393827900